My *Joy* Journey

*How to overcome life's greatest obstacles
and challenges with Joy*

NAOMI JOY NELSON

Interior & Cover Layout & Design:

Tarsha L. Campbell

Published by:

DOMINIONHOUSE

Publishing & Design, LLC

P.O. Box 681938 | Orlando, Florida 32868 | 407.703.4800

www.mydominionhouse.com

First, to my parents, Willie Nelson, Sr. and Theresa Robertson Nelson, you have been my greatest joy for my entire life. Your love for God, the anointing on your ministry, your prayer life, and demonstration of faith inspired me as a child. You have been my best friends my entire life, and I adore you both! The seeds that you have sown are taking root in all of us. Nothing you have sown for the gospel was in vain…your harvest is ready, and it is full!

A very special thank you to my father, for your love and support for my entire life in both music and ministry. Thank you for raising me to be a strong woman and an anointed and skilled musician. I appreciate your sensitivity to the Holy Spirit and how you taught all of us the sincerity of worshipping God.

To my oldest sister, Sarah Joy, you have been an amazing example to me as an older sister, confidant, advisor, manager, and friend. You have also been my closest friend. You are loyal, trustworthy, and important. You have such a spirit of wisdom on you.

God anointed you to lead, and I am so grateful that He has allowed you to lead me.

To my sister, Dr. Martha Joy, you make me laugh like no one else! Your joy is genuine! You inspire me so much! You are such a trailblazer. You are so brilliant and exemplary in everything that you do! You, too, are an amazing older sister who I am blessed to be in the shadow of. Thank you for helping to take care of me. Thank you for being such a wonderful sister. Thank you for finding the humor in everything in life, so we can laugh together. Your laughter is such a gift in my life! What a blessing to have family!

To my brothers, Travis Robertson and Ricky Nelson, you have always loved me tenderly and lovingly protected me. You are caregivers, fathers, husbands, and men who love. I honor you both. To my youngest brother, Willie Nelson, Jr., you were my best friend growing up. You were my best buddy. I love you so very much. We had an amazing childhood together. To my children: Joshua, Jayda, and Jeremiah, I love you. You are the most beautiful people in this world to me. I'm honored to be your mother, and I am so grateful for the gift I have in each of you.

To my extended family in my home state of Louisiana, you are the picture of love. You are everything that embodies the essence and spirit of our great state of Louisiana: amazing and beautiful culture, great food, great music, and history!

May the God of hope fill you
with all joy and peace as you
trust in him, so that
you may overflow with
hope by the power of
the Holy Spirit."

———

Romans 15:13 (NIV)

It would not have been possible to have completed this book without the prayerful support and love from family, friends, and significant relationships that God orchestrated.

Thank you to my parents for the tapestry you helped shape in my life and for putting me on the course of Christianity and my destiny. Thank you, Mama, for being the source of constant guidance, wisdom, prayer, and daily scriptures that you read and taught me daily as led by the Holy Spirit.

Thank you, Daddy, for the anointing that you've carried as long as I've known you and for living out the scriptures so boldly in faith. I don't know another man who has more faith than you. I so deeply admire you, Daddy. Thank you! To my family, I love you. You each have blessed and inspired me. You encourage me and support me in so many ways. What a blessing to have family!

To my former pastor, Benny Hinn, I recognized the Holy Spirit in you when I was just a child. I received the gift of speaking in tongues in your ministry as a kid in elementary school. Your ministry changed my life. You are a general in my life, and I am forever grateful for your ministry.

To my former pastor, Joe Manno, your obedience to the Holy Spirit and sensitivity to Him during your Youth Group services under the leadership of Benny Hinn were the best experiences I had ever experienced in a youth service. We had mini crusade-like atmospheres at the altar. Thank you for your obedience. We experienced God because of your leadership.

To my former pastor, Clint Brown, the psalmist-style worship you led coupled with your teachings on praise were integral in the continual development of my life and ministry. Thank you for pure worship and life-altering praise.

To my former youth pastor, Doug Shackelford, your anointing is so integral. You were such an example of honesty, consistency, and loyalty. You cared for me. You allowed me to begin playing saxophone in your ministry. Thank you for always believing in me, encouraging me, and being such an amazing pastor. The youth trip to Tennessee was amazing!

To Pastor Alex Clattenburg, you have such a pure anointing. You are so sincere, and you keep your eyes on the assignment of souls! What an inspiration of faithfulness and tenaciousness you are! You gave me so many opportunities to minister in your services. You always supported and encouraged me. You always honored my gift. You have an anointing of a true father and genuine shepherd. I'm so glad that God entrusted me to your care.

Thank you to Bishop Delores Duren and Alice B. Washington for your encouragement and support. To Prophet Mary Pitts and Tarsha Campbell, thank you for believing in me and speaking into my life. Thank you for prophetically encouraging me to tell my story, write my book, and minister to others. You are the ministry midwives to the birthing of my ministry.

To my students of Orange County Public Schools, staff, and colleagues, Mr. Rufus Redding, thank you for everything that you taught me and for embracing and encouraging me. To my former professors, directors, and "100" members at Florida A&M University, thank you for the opportunity to lead, to serve, and to grow with you. I have been inspired to teach more, love more, give more, and believe for more.

And those the Lord has rescued will return. They will enter Zion with singing; everlasting joy will crown their heads. Gladness and joy will overtake them, and sorrow and sighing will flee away."

Isaiah 35:10 (NIV)

" *The journey to joy is not only about arriving at the final destination of happiness amid life's many hurdles, bumps, and turns, but in actuality, it is about the beauty of finding joy in every aspect of life.*"

INTRODUCTION

When we think of the word joy, we often think of happiness, excitement, and an exuberance for life. We do not always equate joy with hardship or the labor pains before a birthing. Many times, we think that a joyous experience or a joyful life is a result of many positive experiences coupled with a hopeful expectancy.

The journey to joy is not only about arriving at the final destination of happiness amid life's many hurdles, bumps, and turns, but in actuality, it is about the beauty of finding joy in every aspect of life. We are overjoyed upon receipt of something hoped for, expected, or desired.

We can often experience joy in relationships, in accomplishments, in activities, and in the exchange of love. But what about turbulence and troublesome times as well as unexpected losses? Where is joy then? What happens to a dream deferred? A gift that was lost or stolen? Where is joy in these crushing moments of insurmountable loss?

What I have learned through my experience is that joy is still there. Just like hope and faith, joy is ever present. Although sometimes hard to detect, joy can be found in the midst of everything--- especially in the greatest seasons of loss in life. Delayed gratification oftentimes masks itself as unhappiness or the loss of joy, but this is only a part of the process of arriving at the fullness of joy.

I have discovered that there is a process of overcoming challenges, dealing with various losses, and in the midst of all these things, wanting your dream to become a reality. Like Joseph, the journey to the position of leadership and honor that he once dreamt of was coupled with rejection, abuse, and unexpected delay.

The journey to the promise will many times not only have a hindrance but also discouragement and despair. The key is to not lose heart. Like Joseph, if our suffering is a part of the process in our development, God will not leave us. He will be with you during those most traumatic and isolated times of testing. *My Joy Journey* is a story of how in spite of all of the impediments that I encountered,

I maintained my joy in the Lord, and He gave me hope for living!

It is my sincerest prayer that through my story anyone who has lost hope, found themselves discouraged and not wanting to live anymore, lost faith in God, lost faith and confidence in people, lost hope in life, lost hope and expectancy in love and in the possibility of having success and a prosperous future, will find a picture of what God is able to not only restore but renew completely. Remember this promise in scripture, "And He who sits on the throne said, "Behold, I am making all things new." And He said, "Write, for these words are faithful and true" (Revelation 21:5, NASB).

"From that day forward, I was never the same. I knew that I had been touched by God and that He set me apart. I felt called by Him from that day as well. I knew there was something different that He was doing in me."

CHAPTER 1

THE JOY OF THE LORD

As told to me by my parents, I was delivered into the hands of my father who heard the Lord say to him, "Name her Naomi Joy," and he replied back, "Lord, I don't even know how to spell Naomi!" Nonetheless, my father obeyed, and I was born on April 5th in the home of my parents in Lafayette, Louisiana. My mother said that the Lord said to her "This one will not cause you any pain." And she did not endure intense labor pains with me. She also said that she did not have any fear when delivering me.

After the labor and about one hour of delivery, the largest baby of any of her deliveries, coming in at a whopping ten pounds, finally arrived! Without a doubt, it required much courage and humble obedience on the part of my parents to deliver me naturally in our intimate home setting with only prayers and supplications to God during the birthing process. I am astonished and tremendously grateful for the level of faith my parents demonstrated during my birth.

I remember my earliest days watching my parents lead worship as the worship pastors of a local church in Lafayette, Louisiana called the Christian Teaching Center under the leadership of Dr. Elbert Willis. I have such fond memories of those services as well as the tent revival services my parents held weekly.

I can remember running through the church pews like yesterday and Mama and Daddy singing and preaching on stage. Church and ministry were fun to me, and the revivals were the light of my life. This created a firm foundation of faith for me and helped to shape and mold me into the woman I am today.

Eventually, my parents felt a call of God to move from Louisiana to Orlando, Florida to continue evangelizing and setting up their tent revivals. I remember the changes that I had to adapt to as we transitioned into a new setting and especially into public schools. I really enjoyed my earliest years with my mom as my homeschool teacher.

I loved the lessons in the textbooks and remember flipping delightfully through the books on Mama and Daddy's bed. There was something so special, sacred, and safe about being homeschooled by Mama. We learned in the same home where she baked peach cobbler, and that same sense of warmth and comfort accompanied the teaching I received.

Despite the loss of those experiences, God enabled me to take on the important task of sharing the light of Christ Jesus in a public setting. When I recount the years of my life, my salvation was very early. However, I recall a special service that my father had in Orlando, Florida in one of his tent revivals. My father invited a guest preacher, and this man laid hands on my family and I.

When he laid hands on me, I felt the power of the Holy Ghost go through me, and I trembled, and my hands and arms began to shake. I trembled all the way to the ground until I fainted. I was peacefully laid down, and I remember being flooded with peace as my eyes closed under the many bright tent lights. I laid with my arms outstretched while my family and other guests in the tent revival surrounded me.

There was a reverence and a silence because it was apparent that the Lord had visited us. I had never felt anything like this before nor had a touch from God in that manner.

From that day forward, I was never the same. I knew that I had been touched by God and that He set me apart. I felt called by Him from that day as well. I knew there was something different that He was doing in me. Although I was just a child, He filled me that evening, and my passion for His presence never ceased.

Eventually, my father felt that it was time to put the tent ministry down for a season in order to focus on developing the family more. Daddy spent many nights away from home in his mobile home on the grounds where the tent was located. He felt that being away from home and focusing on the ministry in such a large capacity had to change. During that transition, my father decided to have "home services," and he would still play the piano, sing, and preach, but this time only to us.

My father felt that we still needed to attend Benny Hinn's ministry at Orlando Christian Center (OCC) on Wednesday nights. It was wonderful that we were able to go because we sincerely enjoyed the youth ministry under Pastor Joe Manno. The worship was so anointed, and the messages were so sincere and life changing. I especially remember the altars at the end of each service and how much we felt touched by the Holy Spirit. My sisters and I would worship with our whole hearts, tears streaming down our faces as we experienced the presence of God. He was filling my cup with His glory, and I was being changed by Him all the more.

My parents were very supportive and happy to hear about our wonderful experiences in the services. They encouraged our attendance and supported our hunger for more of God. My parents even supported my desire to be in the main sanctuary for the Sunday services with the adult ministry. I absolutely loved and adored the atmosphere, the worship, the congregation, and the teachings of Pastor Benny Hinn. Although I was a child and would take my baby doll with me into the service, I was drawn to the adult services, and I wanted to be a part of it all.

I remember one service in which Pastor Benny Hinn gave an invitation for everyone who wanted the gift of speaking in tongues to pray a prayer and repeat after him. I remember like yesterday looking up to my mother and saying, "Mama, I want to be able to pray in tongues!" She encouraged me and said, "Just repeat after him in prayer," and I did! I remember my first words in the Spirit too! I was so happy! I felt like I'd won something! I could pray in the Spirit!

From that point on, when we all attended a service together in the main sanctuary, my siblings would look down the pew at me with my hands uplifted, praying in the Spirit. Sometimes they would put their ears near my mouth, so they could hear me and try to comprehend what I was saying. It was peculiar to them, but I kept right on praying. I didn't fully know at the time, but I was being given tools by the Holy Spirit that I would certainly need all the more in the coming years.

All I knew was that I had a hunger for more of God, and if the gift of praying in tongues gave me more intimacy with God, I wanted it! It's for this very reason that I highly encourage and admonish children to "follow the way of love and eagerly desire the gifts of the Spirit, especially prophecy" because the satisfaction that is gained as a result of being filled by God will surpass the things of this world (1 Corinthians 14:1, NIV).

The confidence I gained in the Spirit created a boldness in me, but I was still fully surrendered to my parents. As I matriculated through public school, I gradually came out of my very timid and shy persona and began to boldly demonstrate my faith in the power of God at my school. By the time I reached the fifth grade, I felt a very strong desire to run for the student class president.

I recall praying a prayer and requesting of God, "Lord, give me a platform to display your glory." That prayer, in itself, was a calling and a desire that God had placed in my heart to lead people. I sincerely believe that because of this prayer, God gave me success.

I was elected the fifth-grade student government president. My mom, a teacher's aide at my elementary school, was overjoyed. She was happier than I was! She hugged me so much. It was as if it was her own personal victory. I, on the other hand, was very ill the day of the election. I had never had such a terrible stomachache and pain. It was so bad I wanted to leave school early, but my mom insisted that I stay for the results. The sickness made it difficult to celebrate in that moment, but in my heart, I rejoiced because I had won the victory.

God gave me victory in the area of leadership in my school as well as in my community. God gave me the boldness to share that I could lay hands on the sick and minister to others in spite of being a child when I visited my neighbors' home church. They were proud of me and told their pastor. Although this was unusual, the pastor recognized that God was with me. He instructed me to lay hands on specific people who were sick, so I moved about the entire congregation in absolute boldness and laid hands on everyone he instructed me to. They all fell by the power of the Holy Ghost.

Afterwards, he invited me back to the pulpit in front of his congregation and knelt down before me and asked me to pray for him. I laid my hand upon his head, and I heard the Lord say to me that he was in need of a specific amount of money for his ministry, and I spoke it over him. It was a precious moment handcrafted by God. To my surprise, he asked me to come back and preach. I did not expect that because I was just a child. He addressed me as if I were not.

Under the anointing, it was easy for me to lay hands and pray for the sick. It was easy to pray in the Spirit and operate in the giftings that God had given me. I felt as if I had been doing this my entire life. However, I had never preached a sermon. I agreed and went home tasked with a responsibility that most ten-year-old girls usually don't feel the weight of, but I knelt down on my knees and opened the Bible to search out what the Lord would have me to preach. This is the scripture that I read: "There was a man of the Pharisees named Nicodemus, a ruler of the Jews. The same came to Jesus by night, and said unto him, Rabbi, we know that thou are a teacher come from God: for no man can do these miracles that thou doest, except God be with him. Jesus answered and said unto Him, Verily, verily

I say unto thee, except a man be born again, he cannot see the kingdom of God" (John 3:3, NKJV).

I didn't fully comprehend the scripture and didn't feel fully prepared to preach in that season. I was certainly anointed and called by God, but it simply wasn't my season. God still had to prepare me for public speaking. He had to groom me for leadership.

After all, I still played with my Barbie dolls. I wondered if God would be upset with me if I played with my dolls instead of reading the Bible. I felt pulled in more than one direction. I felt the need to minister to others and the natural desire to be a child. God had his perfect way in that season of my life. He allowed me to continue to play with my dolls, toys, and my little brother, Willie, so I could develop and mature with a healthy balance according to His perfect timing.

The prayer that I prayed about God giving me a platform to display His glory continued to be answered in my life. When God answers prayers, He answers them every day of our lives. His answers are a constant provision in our lives. God honored my prayer and made sure He gave me an opportunity to lead others, so ultimately, I could share the light of Christ Jesus that He put in my life to be seen by others.

God continued to bless me in the area of leadership, and I was later elected student government president in the eighth grade as well as my senior year of high school. God was faithful and answered a prayer that I prayed as a little girl over and over again. He also answered the need to use my voice. Music became my voice of confidence as I matured and developed the ability to share with others.

At Catalina Elementary School, gathered in a school-wide assembly, I saw a small elementary band playing on stage. From the very back of the cafeteria, I could still see the alto saxophone. I knew from that moment, I wanted to play the saxophone. For me, it was love at first sight! I joined the elementary band in hopes of playing the alto saxophone, but instead, I started on the trumpet. I worked on the trumpet until middle school and received a saxophone from my Dad for Christmas.

Playing the saxophone became the starting point for my eventual ministry. I believe that God not only wanted me to become an instrumentalist but also wanted me to develop and gain confidence as a performer and have something to share that would enable me to eventually have a platform as I had so earnestly prayed. Eventually, I began picking up songs "by ear," and my father gave me a Kenny G CD to practice along with. After some time passed, I was able to perform a few songs from the album and shared them with my classmates and teacher.

My band director, Mr. Kenneth Wilkerson, was also a saxophonist who often performed solos in our concerts. He was an amazing musician. He even performed locally. I remember his smile and comments at the conclusion of my performance. He said that I made him so proud and that I reminded him of himself when he was a little kid. He was a great teacher, and under his leadership, our band earned superior ratings with numerous all state and all county student participation.

I still remember when I first joined his class. When I first joined his class, he tested each student at the piano with pitch singing, and when he first heard me sing and match pitch, he said, "You should join chorus" because I sang well and matched pitches accurately. I insisted that I wanted to stay in band, and he supported my decision. For me, that was the best decision! If I had joined chorus, I would never have learned to play the saxophone. Learning to play an instrument was the best direction for me at that time.

God was up to something wonderful in my life. He was allowing music to help me gain confidence and open up. Playing my saxophone made me happy. Making music from my heart in improvisation, worship, and smooth jazz, was a beautiful form of expression that gave me purpose and complimented my introverted personality. God continued to use me and promoted me musically.

After three successful years of band performances and developing as a solo musician, I was ready for high school. I auditioned for drum major at Jones High School. This process was one of the most challenging I ever experienced. The physical workouts, conditioning, marching, and routines were very demanding. Nonetheless, I was selected as a drum major after my initial tryout and audition in the 9th grade.

Being a high school drum major felt like the highest position of leadership that I had ever been given because I was in charge of an entire band of over one hundred students. My high school band director, Mr. Rufus Redding III, respected and entrusted me to lead his students. Because of the confidence and trust that he had in me, I became an even stronger leader. I continued in this leadership role for the next two years and had many wonderful experiences with our performances at what was formerly called the Citrus Bowl.

We had such a great turnout at our games and especially at our annual Jones High School versus Evans High School football game and Battle of the Bands. Many people called it the "Mini-Classic" similar to that of the annual Florida A&M University versus Bethune Cookman University annual Classic Battle of the Bands and football games.

"*A joyful heart is good medicine, but a crushed spirit dries up the bones.*"

———

Proverbs 17:22 (ESV)

" *In that season, I didn't possess enough boldness to stand up against this type of an attack. I was weakened by it. It crushed me emotionally. It changed the way that I looked at myself. It made me wonder if I was a good person.*"

CHAPTER 2

THE LOSS OF JOY

After many wonderful memories, football games, friendships, proms, and academic studies, I decided that I wanted to attend Florida A&M University where I was offered a Presidential Scholarship in the amount of $40,000.00. The scholarship was such a blessing and gave me further hope for my future. I left Orlando fully equipped for my next season of education.

It was a hard transition because I was the very first of my siblings to leave Orlando, Florida for collegiate study. My older sisters and brother attended Valencia Community College, and the girls graduated from UCF, while my brother later attended Liberty University with a full scholarship and later joined the military. I became the only one in the family to attend an HBCU.

During my first year at the university, I started to attend a church that other friends of mine also attended. College life was demanding, exciting, and a totally new world. There were so many young, attractive, collegiate men. I was always marriage-minded and wanted to date the person who I would marry because I wanted to be intentional in my relationships and remain pure until marriage.

I started talking to a young man who didn't share the same convictions as me, and it scared me. I had never been sexually intimate with anyone, but he had. I had attended proms and exchanged innocent kisses, but I had not been in a long-term relationship. I had never been in a setting with a young man that could lead to a major moral compromise. My parents had always protected and monitored me. I was always so preoccupied with music and academic studies that I never really had time for relationships and dating.

I was very concerned about this relationship and was overcome with emotion and fear that I was out of God's will for my life. I decided to attend a prayer service at the church and began to cry during the prayer. One of the ministers, who was leading the prayer service, took note of me and after the service connected with me and gave me his number.

He was trusted among the other collegiate aged females and males, so I, too, felt safe. Little did I know that his "counsel" was corrupted by the lust that he had for young women. What started out as simple "fellowship" was more of an investigation on his part to see what angle he could use to snare me. Much like a snake studies its prey long before it attacks, he was plotting his opportunity to ensnare me.

He took another young lady and me out to eat at a restaurant, and we all talked. When he first picked me up, the other young lady was in the front seat, and I rode in the back. His cologne was strong and stinky. It was unnecessarily strong. It permeated throughout the car. It was too over the top. It was such a turn-off. I didn't know then, but he was trying to project himself on to me or even both of us. I didn't find him physically or in any form attractive.

He was an older man. He was a leader. I wasn't attracted to my leader. I was very attracted to the young man who I was afraid to be involved with any further due to the fear of losing my virginity and what I feared would compromise the anointing on my life. Nonetheless, from that one evening at the restaurant, a relationship ensued.

This minister insisted that I give him my telephone number. He insisted on having every form of contact information that I could provide--even my home telephone number at my parents' home in Orlando, Florida. Initially I didn't feel uneasy about it because I just blindly trusted him as a minister. Besides, my friends also trusted him, so I felt that it would be safe. He called my dormitory room very frequently, and I spoke with him for long periods of time. He would listen intently and provide his thoughts on my dating relationships and various topics that I rambled about. I looked at it as having a mentor and father figure while away at college.

I admired him. He was intellectual, prophetic, and had so much wisdom. The problem, however, was that it was perverted. He would make sexual inferences and use profane words to describe certain things. He described women in the church who cried or became demonstrative and emotional during prayer as women wanting sex. I was alarmed and shocked by his perverted perceptions and some of the things that he said. He was not convicted of this type of perverted thinking and was unapologetic about his profane speech.

During that time, I had a roommate who was not a Christian, and she warned me that this minister who I was speaking to was up to no good. I laughed it off because I trusted him. He was the type of person who would manipulate scriptures and circumstances in order to control innocent young minds. Unfortunately, I had not yet been taught and equipped with how to recognize these types of abusers. In our society, we are generally taught to trust ministers, and we so often give them a pardon because we see them as agents of God.

Although certain things he said made me feel cross, I still continued to listen to him because he said so many more things that were actually biblical and full of wisdom. But that's the problem. Satan knows the scriptures. He knows them quite well! He quotes them as well as God many times! He just manipulates what is holy to benefit himself. He wants to serve his own appetite. He wants to replace God in our lives. This minister became stronger than the voice of the Holy Spirit in my life. That was all a part of Satan's many plans to destroy me. God, however, had a bigger and better plan. My closest friends became concerned with how often he called my cell phone and inquired about it. Much to my surprise and disbelief, my friends made it clear to me that he was a married man. I was in total shock. It was as if the scales fell from my eyes, and I realized that his intentions toward me were completely inappropriate and immoral.

He was trying to slowly pervert me and seduce me into an intimate relationship with him. He was not trying to mentor and counsel me. No wonder he encouraged my relationship with a young man who didn't share my convictions on pre-marital sex. At this revelation, I completely disconnected from him. I ignored all calls and texts. He, however, kept calling relentlessly. It was insane. A normal person would back off. His calling intensified. I was so afraid. I felt so unsafe. I felt so violated.

I felt as if this minister was trying to lead me into adultery with him. Unbeknownst to me, he was using his position to manipulate, abuse, and attempt to have a sexual affair with multiple young women in the church as well as with me! Although no sexual activity of any sort occurred between us, his motives were exposed, and it all made complete sense.

He wanted me to be promiscuous. He wanted me to also be promiscuous with him. I was disappointed, grieved, and very ashamed. Someone who I completely trusted with my prayers, thoughts, emotions, and matters of the heart was trying to have an affair with me.

I returned home to Orlando, Florida and told my parents and family. He continued to call. He started to call our home phone relentlessly. I was so afraid and traumatized. My sister, Martha, picked up the phone and let him know that if he ever called me or our home again, we would expose him to his church. At that, all the calls stopped. I was so thankful for my sister. In that season, I didn't possess enough boldness to stand up against this type of an attack. I was weakened by it. It crushed me emotionally. It changed the way that I looked at myself. It made me wonder if I was a good person.

This sexual harassment and attempt to lure me made me feel that something was wrong with me. I was the victim, but I felt responsible. I was bleeding emotionally. I shared this with almost everyone I trusted. I also shared it with someone who worked at the university. She recommended that I get counseling immediately.

I took her advice, and I did. I went in for counseling, and the counselor wanted me to get rape counseling because according to her, although I was not raped, I shared many of the same feelings of violation that victims of rape endure. I hurt so very badly on the inside, and I wanted to die. I felt so much grief. I couldn't stop crying. I cried so many nights. I felt so alone. I stopped attending the church with my friends because of what happened.

The minister was eventually exposed for this, and it was revealed that he had gone so far as to kiss another young lady. I learned that he was hospitalized shortly after for a major health issue. It still didn't change the damage that he had caused me emotionally. I was broken on the inside, and I saw myself as tainted. My esteem was shattered. I was ashamed. Every time I visited another church, I felt the same way. I wondered, "Is this pastor also going to be attracted to me and try to have an affair with me?" I couldn't join another church for years. I tried my best to move forward from this devastating experience that happened during my freshman year in college. I found myself pursuing the same musical and academic goals that I had in my earlier years but was still very much wounded. I wanted to be loved and instead was abused. I wanted guidance and Godly leadership but was manipulated.

Regardless of the fact that God intervened right in time to prevent a possible rape or sexual affair, I was still very much impacted by the nature of the relationship. The very concept of a person using their ministerial office to entice and manipulate young girls under the guise of a "small group leader" or "counseling" was devastating to me.

I didn't feel comfortable in church anymore. I was hurt, angry, and disappointed in God for allowing this to happen to me. Staying out of church and resenting God for allowing this delayed my healing. I grieved this disappointment but never fully healed. I moved forward but not in wholeness. Eventually, I became engaged and married only to find that I had once again failed to recognize an unhealthy relationship.

You Have to Recognize To Move Forward

I didn't know how to recognize the patterns of unhealthy relationships, abusers and abusive cycles. I couldn't even fully tell what abuse was. I just knew that I felt sincerely afraid for my safety and taken advantage of. I also knew that when I was away, I felt life and joy again. The demonic pull in abusive relationships will steal your joy. It's relentless and restless. It's parasitic and exploitive in every way. Your joy, exuberance, and energy for life will be snatched right out of you.

I had to learn that abuse is not always physical. Sometimes it is an exploitive and manipulative relationship with an inappropriate access or influence that can deter you from your destiny. The effects of this can be very detrimental. This is what inspired me to study this type of spiritual warfare in the next season in search of my joy.

"Rejoice in hope, be patient

in tribulation,

be constant in prayer."

———

Romans 12:12 (ESV)

*Why Lord? Why did this have to happen to me? Why did this have to be my story?"
Similarly, we could easily question why did God allow the young, anointed David to become the hunted? Why is it that the hunger for God leads to being deathly pursued by Satan and all his minions?"*

CHAPTER 3

SEARCHING FOR JOY

At times, I wrestled with God about why He allowed me to endure this, but I decided that although I didn't understand, I was going to trust God fully. My prayer had always been for God to give me a platform to display His glory. As a skilled musician, singer, and an educated and articulate speaker, my natural talents and abilities would seem efficient enough for such a platform, but God had another plan. God, many times, will use our broken pieces to help others come into wholeness.

In doing so, we, too, find our healing. After all, the scripture says, "He who waters others will himself be watered" (Proverbs 11:25, NASB). There is much truth to this word. I have already experienced it in sharing my story with women in conferences. But the questions of why attacks and losses come is what I believe God allows in order to strengthen us in our Christian walk.

I personally believe that an anointing on your life is going to attract a certain level of demonic attack. We can observe the life of David and how Saul was relentless in his pursuit of destroying and killing him. Although David was called to minister to Saul, Saul was used by Satan in an attempt to sabotage David's kingship. The attack was on the future of Israel, God's seed.

The seed is always where Satan launches his primary attack. He used Pharaoh to kill all male, Hebrew boys in order to destroy the prophecy of the soon coming deliverer (Moses), and he used Herod to kill all the male boys in order to destroy the Messiah, Jesus Christ, in his infancy. Although my greatest attacks happened as I matured into a young woman versus as an infant, it was my ministerial infant stage that Satan was trying to sabotage.

This still leads me to ask, "Why Lord? Why did this have to happen to me? Why did this have to be my story?" Similarly, we could easily question why did God allow the young, anointed David to become the hunted? Why is it that the hunger for God leads to being deathly pursued by Satan and all his minions? Why does God allow us to be abused? Why does God allow us to be on the run for our lives?

We should delve deeper and begin to ask specific question such as: What is God birthing out of me during this season? What are the roots (if any) in my life or childhood that have helped orchestrate a path to my destruction? Do I know and can I identify the specific spiritual attack or lie of Satan on my life, my family, my home, and my future generation?

These questions are important to ask God in order to receive answers and clarity. All of the answers can be found in the Word of God. He has already answered in scripture. Consider reading both the book of Job and Ephesians 6:10-18 as well as 2 Corinthians 10:3-4 for insight into overcoming hard trials of life and scriptural encouragement during spiritual warfare.

My search for truth and the restoration of my joy began in the season when I was a single mother, living alone in an apartment with my three children. I decided the summer after my divorce to seek the Lord with my whole heart and return to him completely."

CHAPTER 4

HEALING AND RESTORATION OF JOY

After surviving ministerial abuse that severely wounded me followed by a marriage coupled with multiple separations, and then reconciliations that soon led to separations again, and custody battles, I needed God more than ever. God created a time and space for me to seek Him fully and allow Him to reveal Himself to me in an intimate and personal way. It was necessary to get the answers to the questions in my life that I so deeply needed. A new season of healing awaited me. It was a fresh start for me. I was on a journey of a new life with my children. Although this was a very scary time for me, God was with me.

This had proven to be the fight of my life…running from the attacks, protecting my children, and refusing to be abused. It's no wonder that I fell in love with the Psalms and the story of Saul's pursuit of David. The enemy wants to destroy what God has anointed and rob you of the joy of your salvation.

The enemy wants to have you running for fear of your life. The enemy wants to rob you of your peace, your joy, your freedom, and your strength. However, this fight made me strong. I became a warrior. God taught me how to war in the Spirit with prayer.

God taught me how to own my truth, to not shy away from calling what I had endured abuse, to speak up about it, to tell my story, and to surround myself with people who supported me and knew the truth and the truth of God. He used many people to help me in my deliverance. I am forever indebted to them, and I know that God has a reward for them.

My search for truth and the restoration of my joy began in the season when I was a single mother, living alone in an apartment with my three children. I decided the summer after my divorce to seek the Lord with my whole heart and return to him completely. I had always been a Christian and sought the Lord, but this time, I promised the Holy Spirit that I was going to rededicate myself to Him.

This was a beautiful promise that the Lord honored. It gave Him permission to access my soul in the places where I was wounded and hid from Him. It put me back into complete submission to Him. It was during that season of prayer that I got up at 5 a.m. and would lay prostrate on my floor in prayer. My children were fast asleep, so I had these life-changing and amazing mornings with God. During that time, I played worship music and prayed in the Spirit. I had lengthy conversations with God and shared the contents of my heart. I repented for wrong thinking and areas in my life where I didn't trust God.

I was in a soul-cleansing season, and God was healing me. I also desired to grow more in the knowledge of God. I experienced so much joy in seeking God that I earnestly wanted to learn so much more! In earlier years, I had ministered to others and performed prophetic music on my instrument in which a supernatural sound (orchestrated by the Holy Spirit) came out of my instrument, and the service was significantly impacted. It was an honor to be used by God.

I remember observing people next to me fall under the power of the Holy Spirit and witnessed the miraculous! These signs and wonders inspired and amazed me. I was so eager and excited for the next season of experiencing the supernatural. But the Lord was concerned about the condition of my soul. It was in this season of seeking the Lord that I came to know Him even more personally as I worshipped and sought Him in my home.

In this season of seeking the Lord in my home, my joy was being restored. The joy that I had was the joy of the Lord! This perhaps was what God was seeking to restore in me. Not only did I need emotional and spiritual healing, but I needed to trust the Lord again fully with my heart, so that I could experience the joy and freedom of living in His love once again. My childhood relationship with God brought me sincere joy. I was happy, healthy, and whole because of the salvation that I found in Jesus Christ. My adoration for Him was easily shared and expressed in music, and I sincerely loved performing music both in educational settings and especially in worship to God.

In my earlier years as a teen, I dreamt that I was in heaven, bowed down to the ground laying prostrate on the floor in surrender. I saw Jesus seated on the throne with elders seated next to Him. He was at the center and was elevated over the men seated next to him. The other men who were seated next to him had various robe colors and adornments which represented the honor that they had received for performing great exploits while ministering on earth.

In that dream, Jesus was a beautiful man who had just been crucified and given this seat in heaven. Time was so different in the heavenly realm. While on earth this had occurred over 2,000 years ago, in heaven, this had just happened! Jesus sat with all authority. He didn't have to utter one word to me. I knew who He was. I recognized His majesty. He and the elders spoke to one another. I could never lift myself from the ground. I hid my face from Him much like the prophet, Isaiah, who cried, "Lord I am undone…for mine eyes have seen the King, the Lord of hosts!" I, too, was overwhelmed and also cried, "Lord, send me back! Lord, send me back!"

When I awoke from the dream, I leaped off of the sofa in excitement to share this with my family. It was this experience and the supernatural experiences that surrounded it that stayed with me for many years, and I cherished it in my heart. This brought the joy of the Lord to me! The joy that I had because of this experience was sharing about what I observed and learned.

It was many years later that I had another dream in which I dreamt that I saw Jesus. I was walking on the sidewalk in a major city that looked like a downtown business area with many people walking to and fro in the opposite direction. It was strikingly similar to the walking traffic of a major city like New York City. There were possibly hundreds of people walking in various directions but in the midst of everything, I saw Jesus! He was clothed in a white or tan colored linen robe, and He had a veil over His face. I immediately recognized Him and ran fast towards Him in excitement. When I arrived to meet Him, I exclaimed, "My Lord!" and I hugged Him. My joy was complete.

"As the Father has loved me, so have I loved you. Now remain in my love. If you keep my commands, you will remain in my love, just as I have kept my Father's commands and remain in his love. I have told you this so that my joy may be in you and that your joy may be complete" (John 15:9-11, NIV). This is the joy of the Lord: to reconcile us to God.

This is why in my dream Jesus was so intent and very concerned about the state of the world. He was concerned about the people and how they were so busy going about their lives and affairs that they did not see Him in the midst of them, but they also were not ready for His return. In my excitement, I asked Him, "What can I do for you?!?!" He said, "Tell them I am coming." That's all He said.

In my dream, I took off running as fast as I could in the opposite direction from where He stood. I had to tell all the people who had passed Him that He was coming. This was a calling dream. This was an assignment. Although His face was veiled, I consider it another vision of Jesus. These visions and dreams inspired me. They gave me great joy and hope for His return!

The scripture echoes this perfectly in Revelation 22:20 (NIV), "He who testifies to these things says, "Yes, I am coming soon. Amen. Come Lord Jesus." These earlier seasons of receiving revelations and dreams of encountering Jesus were different from what my next season would entail. In my next season, Jesus revealed Himself to me as my Healer. He became my Counselor. He became my Help. I sought the Lord in prayer as the scriptures declare in Jeremiah 29:13-14 (NIV), "You will seek Me and find Me when you seek me with all your heart. I will be found by you declares the Lord."

I wanted God to give me revelations and dreams. I wanted supernatural experiences to bring me joy in Him again. But in this season, as a newly divorced mother of three small children, I did not have dreams of Jesus, but I received healing. It was during this time that I learned the person of the Holy Spirit and that He is gentle. He loved me and wanted to restore me. "He heals the brokenhearted and binds up their wounds" (Psalm 147:3, NIV).

I was reminded of the scripture, "The Spirit of the Lord is upon me because he has anointed me to proclaim good news to the poor, He has sent me to proclaim freedom for the parishioners and recovery of sight for the blind, to set the oppressed free" (Luke 4:18, NIV). From this scripture, I felt the comfort and presence of the meekest man in all the earth.

Jesus promises in scripture, "Take my yoke upon you and learn from me, for I am gentle and humble in heart, and you will find rest for your souls" (Matthew 11:19, NIV).

This scripture came to life to me personally and confirmed that Jesus is a compassionate, loving, and gentle man who is perfectly called the Lamb of God. John prophetically announced and described Him best in scripture, "The next day he saw Jesus coming to him and said, "Behold the Lamb of God who takes away the sin of the world." Jesus, this perfect Lamb, personally addressed my fears of allowing anyone to get close to my heart again. Jesus came to restore my soul. He came to bring me internal healing. He came to tell me who He is: gentle. The Lord wanted access into the places in my soul. He wanted to heal the brokenness in me.

Jesus revealed himself and confirmed His identity through the scriptures to me. He made the scriptures come alive. He was everything the Word said about Him . . . He was personable. His purpose is to bring healing to the soul through rest and surrender to Him. His desire is to see the broken places within us healed and restored. I wanted more encounters, more experiences, and a greater level of the anointing to rest upon me.

While Jesus did grant these things, His heart was to bring inner healing to me. I sought Christian counseling which was very helpful, and I sought the wisdom and advice from my parents and other trusted leaders which was also very helpful. I am an advocate for counseling and seeking out instruction from trusted leaders. After all, the scriptures advise, "Without good direction, people lose their way; the more wise counsel you follow, the better your chances" (Proverbs 11:14, MSG).

The Lord led me to many people who gave me advice, shared their stories of abuse, their testimonies of freedom, prayed with me, led me through deliverance prayers, and offered hope and support for me. But Jesus came to fully heal me. Jesus came to note the condition of my soul, to bring to my attention that the emotional wounds were still unhealed and that I needed Him to fully restore me. I also needed to trust Him to touch the raw places within me that I shielded from Him. He was grieved at my condition. He was hurt that I didn't trust that He wouldn't cause me pain. He was sincerely grieved that I guarded certain places in my soul from Him.

Like in my dream, many times we not only do not see or recognize Him, but we also are not prepared for Him. This is the most grievous thing to the Lord. In Luke chapter 19, verse 41, in the Message version, Jesus weeps over the people of Jerusalem saying, "If you had only recognized this day, and everything that was good for you!" He wept over the tragic loss of opportunity of salvation and healing for their souls.

The scriptures tell us that "The Lord is not slow in keeping His promise, as some understand slowness. Instead He is patient with you, not wanting anyone to perish, but everyone to come to repentance" (2 Peter 3:9, NIV). He sincerely does not want any of us to miss His coming or His personal call of salvation and healing.

"This is good and acceptable in the sight of God our Savior, Who will have all men to be saved, and to come unto the knowledge of the truth. For there is one God, and one mediator between God and man, the man Jesus Christ, Who gave himself a ransom for all, to be testified in due time" (1 Timothy 3:2-6, NASB).

God sent His son, Jesus, to be a propitiation for our sins, to pay the price for our suffering, to be the ransom for our lives. He never intended abuse to be our portion in this life. Inevitably suffering will occur as a Christian, but only suffering that He purposes. When suffering occurs, He comes to restore and heal. He is a gentle Healer. I compare my experiences to that of a child with a freshly skinned knee with a raw, open wound where the blood and flesh are exposed. If a parent, in a desire to address the wound, reaches to touch the child's knee, the child may jerk backwards in fear of further pain being brought to the wound.

It requires patience and loving kindness to assure a wounded child that although they are wounded, the parent is there to bring healing and properly address their wound to care for it so it can be restored. The sight of the wound, the condition of it, the current sting, the racing and beating of the heart, and the fear and trauma that accompany this experience make it very difficult for the wounded child to trust even a loving parent.

Unfortunately, even the cleansing of the wound will be painful until the work is done, but during that process, there is faith in a loving caregiver like Jesus who sincerely desires to bring complete healing. This very process was necessary for me. I had to go on a journey of healing with Jesus. The one encounter was not the Band-aid over my wound or a one-time fixer upper. Internal soul wounds take time to heal, and I had more visitations and conversations with Jesus in order to mend the broken and fragmented pieces in my soul.

On another visitation from the Lord, He spoke to me regarding more things in my heart that I needed to surrender to Him. He spoke plainly and directly to me and said, "Grief is Mine." It was then that I realized that grief had become an idol (amongst other things that the Lord had revealed) in my heart.

The grief that I cleaved to for the loss of a marriage, singleness, single motherhood, loss of cherished possessions, and the shame of my situation were more significant to me in a place in my heart than God. It is completely normal to grieve. While we are supposed to grieve and mourn our losses, the scriptures tell us there is a time and season to everything.

To everything there is a season, and a time to every purpose under the heaven: A time to be born, and a time to die; a time to plant, and a time to pluck up that which is planted; A time to kill, and a time to heal; a time to break down, and a time to build up; A time to weep, and a time to laugh; a time to mourn, and a time to dance; A time to cast away stones, and a time to gather stones together; a time to embrace, and a time to refrain from embracing; A time to get, and a time to lose; a time to keep, and a time to cast away; A time to rend, and a time to sew; a time to keep silence, and a time to speak; A time to love, and a time to hate; a time of war, and a time of peace (Ecclesiastes 3:1-8, KJV).

Seasons are a part of the orchestration of life. Seasons are the tapestry of Christ Jesus in each experience in life. The problem, however, comes when we stay in a season for too long. Grief too, has a season. We are supposed to move forward and onward toward the high calling in Christ Jesus. We are supposed to trust Him on this new journey!

"He said to another man, "Follow me." But he replied, "Lord first let me go and bury my father." Jesus said to him, "Let the dead bury the dead, but you go and proclaim the kingdom of God." Still another said, "I will follow you, Lord; but first let me go back and say goodbye to my family." Jesus replied, "No one who puts a hand to plow and looks back is fit for service in the Kingdom of God" (Luke 9:59-62, NIV).

We are supposed to take a step each and every day, knowing that like God provided a pillar of fire by night and the cloud by day and manna from heaven and birds of the air for meat for His chosen people, we, too, will be provided for. When Jesus calls us to leave the weights and idols of grief and loss, He wants us to by faith surrender these things to Him and follow Him into a season of healing, restoration, calling, and purpose in Him.

Scripture References:

Matthew 11:28-29

Isaiah 42:2

Matthew 21:5

" *Don't feel discouraged or isolated. God is with you! God is always fighting for us. God is always on our side! There will always be a necessity for God in our lives. There will always be an area where we need His divine help to receive deliverance and healing.* "

CHAPTER 5

Spiritually Equipped To Maintain Joy

Sometimes when we grieve our past misfortunes, we doubt God and make an idol out of a sad or disappointing circumstance or situation in our lives. Jesus is supposed to be Lord of our lives and the Lord of our hearts. Grief has its season, but it doesn't permanently belong in our hearts---Jesus does! In this next season of the Lord's revelation to me, I had to surrender my sorrows to Him.

I had to stop mourning yesterday and trust Him with today and tomorrow. Today and tomorrow are much better than yesterday! Hope is here! Jesus is in the now moments! He is the keeper of time and the ruler of our hearts! He wants the very best for us and in us. We have to surrender and confess to God all of the contents of our hearts. Many times, we serve and worship God but don't surrender everything to Him.

Sometimes we not only hide our wounds but our sins as well. God is fully aware of this. Many of our sins are the result of our hidden unaddressed wounds. When we expose ourselves fully to God, He can begin the healing process with us. This is also a part of our deliverance. God sincerely desires that we are healed, delivered, and set free.

Sometimes God allows an adversary or an attack from Satan to prepare us for the spiritual battle that is waging against us. Many times, we are anointed in our youth and equipped with the gifting for the assignment that God has called us to, but we are not yet prepared for battle. Take David, for example, as the young shepherd boy who was in an "in between" season where he was at the precipice of war to kingship.

David was anointed by the prophet, Samuel, over all of his brothers. He had experience in warfare. He defeated a lion and a bear in defense of the sheep he had been entrusted to care for. He had even come to the battleground prepared to defend the name of his God against Goliath. When Saul attempted to put his armor on David, it didn't fit. In the natural, David didn't need Saul's armor because he had been equipped by God to fight the giant and defeat him supernaturally. But in the natural, David was not quite ready to be the king based on one victory over Goliath. That, undeniably, must be a very humbling experience, yet David was a humble servant. He didn't show any signs of pride or delight in his personal honor or achievements. He had no coat, like Joseph, with many colors to wear and showcase for all to see. Although anointed for battle and leadership of a nation, the armor of a king did not fit him yet. Many times, we are called and anointed to a mission or battlefield but not yet appointed. Sometimes there are forthcoming battles necessary to build our muscles. The battles are necessary to strengthen and develop us to fit the armor appropriate for a king.

The transition from a shepherd boy to a king was a process of many, many wars. I can somewhat relate to that when I was a young girl who ferociously and fearlessly proclaimed the good news of the gospel. God was developing me into a seasoned warrior who could defend a nation. (My nation is my children, my people, my family, my leadership, my region: whatever city, state, country, or nation that God appoints to me in the Spirit.)

In order to be trusted with these things, we first must be tested. In addition to dreams and visions of Jesus, I had warfare dreams. The dreams symbolized what I was fighting and overcoming in the natural realm but first had to be accomplished in the Spirit realm. I dreamt that I was trapped in a house with a woman. The woman represented a demonic spirit that had a hold over me. I could not leave the house.

I was standing in the house, and she was standing near me. There was a large dog, possibly a Rottweiler, that had my wrist in his mouth, holding me captive. I could not get free. Something happened in that dream and miraculously, I was freed. I walked right out of that house! When I walked out of the house, a line of beautiful people in fine clothes were surrounding the house. I understood the dream to mean that I had been delivered from the spirit that held me captive, and because I had been set free, I was able to free so many other people!

The people looked like redeemed saints. They looked dressed for Sunday morning service. They were beautiful! I see why God loves us so much! They looked like people of God, every race, gender, ethnicity, and culture. All beautiful people of God who He saved through my deliverance. That's the beauty of deliverance. It's not just for you! It's for the people who God has assigned to you. We all have an assignment on the earth. We all have people assigned to us.

God uses dreams many times to speak to us. In the book of Job, it reads in chapter 33, verse 13 through 18 "So why do you challenge God to answer you? God speaks in different ways, and we don't always recognize his voice. Sometimes in the night, he uses terrifying dreams to give us warnings. God does this to make us turn from sin and pride and to protect us from being swept away to the world of the dead" (CEV).

That's a good God! A God who loves us enough to KEEP speaking to us! To KEEP pursuing us! Oh, how I love Him! How compassionate is He to protect us from the enemy, forewarn us, and protect us even from ourselves!

Many times, I have had dreams where I see snakes. They vary in size, color, shape, and respond differently in each dream. Once I dreamt that God (in the form of my father) spoke to me about the wonders and amazing and creative things that He had planned for my life and then suddenly, an enormous, yellow python lunged at me directly in my face. It appeared to be contained in a glass cage in the museum but was not. The dream was so vivid and frightening. In fear, I jumped and awoke out of my sleep.

The attack is about what is yet to come, but we do not fear the enemy or his tactics or schemes. We prepare for battle because the enemy is subject to us! In Luke 10:18-19, Jesus assures us that we have been given power over darkness and the enemy.

"I saw Satan fall from heaven like lightning from heaven. I have given you authority to trample on snakes and scorpions and to overcome all the power of the enemy; nothing will harm you. However, do not rejoice that the spirits submit to you, but rejoice that your names are written in heaven" (Luke 10:18-20, NIV). In His love and graciousness, God has often times revealed a snake to me immediately before an attack. I have dreamt of such an attack, and then within one to three days, I've had to kill an actual snake attempting to get into my home or attack me or one of my children. As a result of this ongoing demonic warfare, I have gained confidence in the Spirit. I cleave to Jesus' words of truth that no power in hell has dominion over me or my children. With this confidence, a boldness is birthed in me.

David had boldness to defeat Goliath. He also had tremendous faith in his God. He knew that he was on the side of truth in defending the name of God against a blasphemous enemy. Our real enemy is Satan. Goliath was a giant used by Satan to intimidate and ultimately destroy the nation of Israel. We do not fear our enemy. We prepare for battle. The manner in which we prepare is in the Spirit. We must seek the face of God in prayer and search the scriptures for His instructions. We must still ourselves to hear His still, small voice (1 Kings 19:12).

During the tests and trials of life as well as the many spiritual warfare battles, the Bible provides a war strategy. It gives me personal insight on how to protect every area where I have spiritual dominion: my body, my children and family, my home, my workplace, my community, my relationships, my friendships, and whatever else God entrusts me with. The Bible can be described as a love story about Jesus and His bride (the church) which is the summation of the Song of Solomon, describing Christ Jesus' longing for His church. It can also be described as a war manual with strategies and biblical stories in which God caused His people to triumph over the enemy.

Covenant Christian relationships and a church community is also God's design for His children to combat spiritual warfare. Remember, if you are facing a battle, you are not in the battle alone. In the natural, David fought Goliath alone, but he had an entire army behind him and all of heaven as well as the angelic realm.

While we are able to conquer the enemy in prayer, through fasting, and reading and finding answers in the Word of God, we can still be troubled and tormented in other areas of our lives. Imagine David constantly running from Saul. Imagine the fear that he must have dealt with knowing that this same man who he loved threw a spear at him in an attempt to kill him and in the very home that he loved and ministered to him in. David lovingly served Saul.

David ministered to him in song and skillfully on his instrument. David was despised and hated by Saul because Saul had been rejected by God. David was still innocent of any wrongdoing towards Saul. But the torment must have been tremendous as he constantly fled from him. My point in sharing this is to bring revelation to the fact that although God can and will deliver us, many times, the effects of war still loom over us.

Post-traumatic stress disorder is a very common result of being in a war. I had traumatizing effects from abuse. I started having panic attacks and didn't know what it was. The first time I experienced it, I left work immediately for an emergency doctor visit. The entire time, I thought I was having a heart attack. It was so severe and real.

The pain was exactly what was described as a heart attack. It was then that my doctor said that he wanted to prescribe Ambien for me. I was so disturbed. After running the EKG on me, he determined that it was necessary. I pleaded with him because I don't like taking any drugs, and I would rather take an aspirin a day if that would help. In my pride, I simply couldn't accept a medical prescription for the treatment of anxiety/depression/panic disorders.

I was so ashamed. I was embarrassed. My doctor informed me that many times anxiety is a result of inner traumas as well as stressors in life. I decided to listen to him. When I picked up my prescription, the young man who handed me the prescription looked at me in complete disbelief. He didn't have to say anything.

I knew what he was thinking. It was obvious. I was young and healthy looking. I thought the same things, but I had to realize that it was okay to get help both spiritually and medically for that season. The aspirin or ibuprofen didn't take away my constant chest pains, anxiety, and intense fears. The medicine prescribed actually helped me. Sometimes more than other times, but it did help.

My anxiety and trouble sleeping were rooted in fear. Undoubtedly, stress played some part because I was working full-time and caring for three little children alone. But I had to learn to accept both natural and spiritual help. My mother gave birth to me without the aid of any doctor, nurse, or midwife. My parents intentionally had home births as a way to demonstrate their devotion and confidence in God.

They were under an amazingly anointed pastor in Lafayette, Louisiana by the name of Elbert Willis. He had never relied on medication or even taken an aspirin for pain. His faith-style teaching resembled that of Kenneth Hagin, and my parents were tremendously impacted by his ministry. They served as the worship pastors for the ministry and were very devoted to the teachings. I believed in the healing power of God over medicine but also believed that God could use medicine to help me too.

I had to overcome this embarrassment to recognize that there are so many people my age and younger who battle things like this, and there is no reason to feel embarrassed or ashamed. That is a trick of the enemy to keep you from getting free. While for a season I needed to take the medication more frequently, I no longer require the use of the medication.

I feel that I have completely overcome that battle, but there are other battles that come along with the fight for freedom and victory. Some people are set free from addictions, but they still have to deal with the temptations of being lured back into that lifestyle. These may be called triggers. I have to address triggers in my heart and life that lead to fear, sleepless nights, depression, and anxiety. When I address these triggers in my heart by presenting my brokenness and wounds fully to God for cleansing and healing, I can find freedom again and most importantly, overcoming joy.

Don't feel discouraged or isolated. God is with you! God is always fighting for us. God is always on our side! There will always be a necessity for God in our lives. There will always be an area where we need His divine help to receive deliverance and healing. Even if God brings about the healing coupled with medicine for a season, it will not be forever. Even if you have to go through chemotherapy while in devout prayer for your total healing, God can and will still heal you. He is the God of a second chance.

He wants to heal us in every area of our lives. He wants to make us free. He promised in His word, "I am the God that healeth thee." Exodus 15:26 says, "If you listen carefully to the Lord your God and do what is right in His eyes, if you pay attention to His commands and keep all His decrees, I will not bring on you any of the diseases I brought on

the Egyptians, for I am the Lord, who heals you."
Ultimately, God wants a people after His own heart.
He wants to bring us closer to Him. Psalm 24:3-5
asks, "Who may ascend the mountain of the Lord?
Who may stand in his holy place? The one who has
clean hands and a pure heart, who does not trust
in an idol or swear by a false god. They will receive
blessing from the Lord and vindication from God
their Savior. They will receive the Lord's blessing
and have a right relationship with God their Savior."

God is on our side! He wants us to win. He
always causes us to triumph! 2 Corinthians
2:14 reminds us, "But thanks be to God, who in
Christ always leads us in triumphal procession,
and through us spreads the fragrance of
the knowledge of Him everywhere (ESV).

My joy journey has been riddled with both triumph and tragedy, exuberance and misery, but I have not lost my hope. I have not lost my joy. I am encouraged. It is my goal to live my life as a testament of what God can and will do through a broken vessel."

CHAPTER 6

OVERCOMING WITH JOY

As I reflect upon my past experiences, both triumphant and traumatic, I am reminded that the necessity of trouble and testing as well as favor and blessing are an integral part of shaping our lives and making us more like Christ. Ultimately, our journey is to become more like Him and less of ourselves. If He suffered, we will suffer. But I have confidence in the scripture in 2 Timothy 2:12 that says, "If we suffer, we shall also reign with him: if we deny him, he also will deny us." I am encouraged all the more by this scripture: "For which cause we faint not; but though our outward man perish, yet the inward man is renewed day by day. For our light affliction, which is but for a moment, worketh for us a far more exceeding and eternal weight of glory; While we look not at the things which are seen, but at the things which are not seen: for the things which are seen are temporal; but the things which are not seen are eternal" (2 Corinthians 4:16, KJV).

In my winning season, I decree and declare the Word of God over my life and the lives of my children. I walk by faith and not by sight. I present my requests and the desires of my heart to God. I move from asking to taking authority to commanding the blessings that are already mine over my children, ministry, business, and my life. I minister hope to others by faith in the scripture that as I water others I, too, will be watered. Proverbs 11:25 in the Amplified version encourages us, "The generous man [is a source of blessing and] shall be prosperous *and* enriched, And he who waters will himself be watered [reaping the generosity he has sown]." I am encouraged in Christ, His love, faithfulness, and provision for me and my family.

Life will present unexpected troubles and attacks. It is a part of the Christian life to have a degree of suffering, trials, and tribulations. I am reminded of this powerful word in 2 Corinthians 4:8-18 (KJV):

We are troubled on every side, yet not distressed; we are perplexed, but not in despair; Persecuted, but not forsaken, cast down, but not destroyed; Always bearing about in the body the dying of the Lord

Jesus, which the life also of Jesus might be made manifest in our body. For we which live are always delivered unto death for Jesus' sake, that the life also of Jesus might be made manifest in our mortal flesh. So, then death worketh in us, but life in you. We having the same spirit of faith, according as it is written, I believed, and therefore have I spoken; we also believe, and therefore speak; Knowing that he which raised up the Lord Jesus shall raise up us also by Jesus, and shall present us with you. For all things are for your sakes, that the abundant grace might through the thanksgiving of many redound to the glory of God. For which cause we faint not; but though our outward man perish, yet the inward man is renewed day by day. For our light affliction, which is but for a moment, worketh for us a far more exceeding and eternal weight of glory; While we look not at the things which are seen, but at the things which are not seen: for the things which are seen are temporal; but the things which are not seen are eternal.

My joy journey has been riddled with both triumph and tragedy, exuberance and misery, but I have not lost my hope. I have not lost my joy. I am encouraged. It is my goal to live my life as a testament of what God can and will do through a broken vessel. Today, I own a four-bedroom home in Florida and manage my personal ministry and professional music service. I am an author, educator, and musician, raising three happy, healthy, intelligent, God-fearing children. I am continuing my education as well as pursuing other dreams and goals.

My joy journey has taught me that you can still win in this life in spite of hardships. You can achieve your goals. God is with you, and He will strengthen you to do His will. It is in His will that you prosper and have success. God smiles when He sees His children glorifying Him through the gifts that He gave them. Be encouraged in the Lord! The best is yet to come in Christ Jesus! Victory IS ours! Take heart, Jesus has overcome the world! Remember John 16:33 (NIV), "I have told you these things, so that in me you may have peace. In this world you will have trouble. But take heart! I have overcome the world."

It is my sincere and earnest prayer that you have been both blessed and inspired through the reading of this book. Most importantly, I pray that you have an opportunity to accept Jesus Christ as your Lord and Savior who will also personally minister the hope and healing to you as He has done for me. As a result, you will find your fullest joy in Him. Below is a Salvation and Deliverance Prayer that I welcome you to read and pray to Jesus Christ:

Lord Jesus, I ask that you forgive me for all the mistakes that I have made in my life. Forgive me for wrong relationships, wrong conversations, wrong connections and heal me from traumas and pains of abuse that I may have experienced. Help me to forgive everyone who has abused or harmed me. Set me free from the fear of accepting love and being loved by you. I invite you as Savior into my life and surrender my bad habits, evil motives, and my shortcomings to you. I invite you to make me new again. I thank you that you have cleansed me of all unrighteousness. I thank you that I am healed because you died on the cross for my sins and redeemed me from death. I thank you that I no longer have to endure the pains of abuse because you were wounded for me. I surrender all inappropriate relationships to you and invite you to be the most significant relationship in my life. I welcome God-fearing people who profess Jesus Christ as their Lord and savior into divine fellowship with me. Lord Jesus, I thank you for the healing of my soul, your supernatural joy that replaces grief, and your word of truth that you speak to me. I am saved, healed, and delivered to help others find this joy as I have found in you. Equip me to strengthen and help others as you have helped me in Jesus' name, Amen.

Naomi Joy Nelson is a multi-talented instrumentalist, educator, author and speaker on a mission to liberate, educate, and motivate others through her personal experience. Trained as both a Musician and Educator with a ministerial background, Naomi combines her love of outreach, music and education into a harmonious presentation. A graduate of Florida A&M University, highly sought out musician, minister, and speaker, Naomi has been a voice of inspiration to many. She has engaged hundreds of audiences, students, and is a multi-talented instrumentalist, educator, author and speaker.

You are welcome to email or write the author with comments about this book. You are also welcome to contact her for bookings. Naomi is available for book club presentations, book signings, or speaking engagements for your group or organization (conferences, workshops, retreats, seminars, women's groups, women's ministries and women's clubs).

Contact her at:

800-760-0284
P.O. Box 1515
Apopka, FL 32704

Bookingfornaomijoy@gmail.com
www.naomijoymusic.com

Connect with her on social media:

Facebook:
Https://www.facebook.com/naomi.nelson8

Facebook Page:
Naomijoyjourney

Twitter:
naomijoyjourney

Instagram:
naomijoyjourney